Peter and his Mouse Friends

Ann Sawyer

Principal Lecturer in Early Years Education,
Worcester College of Higher Education
Member of The National Curriculum Working Party for Maths

Illustrated by
Paul Howard

It's 7 o'clock. Time to get up.

How many toys does Peter have?

How many mice are there?

Why not try this with your clothes?

I'm going to build a house.

What shapes can you find at home?
Sort them into sets.

Try building with different shapes.

What picture can you make using the shapes?

A game for as many players as you like.

How many knives, forks and spoons are needed for **2** people? **3** people? **4** people?

Set a table and see.

Monday Tuesday Wednesday Thursday

Friday Saturday Sunday

What day is it?
What is the weather like?
How many days are shown on the chart?
Make your own weather chart for a week.

I'm the tallest.

I'm taller.

I'm tall.

How wide is the bedroom?

How wide is your bedroom?

Who is the tallest in your family?
Who has the longest feet in your family?

PARENTS' GUIDE

Peter and his mouse friends

Maths 5 to 6 years

Dear Parent,

All the activities in Peter and his Mouse Friends are firmly based on the National Curriculum's Programmes of Study and the Attainment Targets set out in the Core Subject Mathematics. The activities are structured in such a way that they correspond directly to the levels of attainment which your child is likely to reach within Key Stage 1.

The book focusses upon the home, its surroundings and situations which are likely to be familiar to your child. There are mathematical investigations for your child to try, problem-solving activities, number, shape, measuring, patterning and data-handling situations.

This pull-out section provides a list of further activities and opportunities for extending and reinforcing the areas already introduced in the child's book.

The games and activities should be enjoyed by your child. Keep them fun and keep the time allotted to each activity short. Young children are only able to concentrate for short periods and impatience and pressure from parents will kill their interest, enthusiasm and curiosity.

As far as possible, everything should be done by the child and adults should resist the temptation to take over the activity. The important thing is for the model, picture or investigation to be the child's own work. The adult's role should be a supporting one, talking to the child, listening to her, encouraging the asking and answering of questions about the activity.

The pronoun 'she' has been used in this section but the activities are equally suitable for boys and girls.

A

Number attainment targets 1 to 5

Counting
pages 3, 8–11, 28–29, 32

The book contains many counting activities. Your child should be encouraged to make estimates of "How many?" before counting. Estimates, by their nature, are not right or wrong; your child will improve her accuracy in estimating, with practice.

Estimating and calculating
pages 24–25

How many?

You will need:
Strong paper bag:
Marbles or dried peas or buttons.

This is a game for all the family. Take it in turns to take a handful of marbles from the bag. Estimate how many, then count. Try making a chart to show your estimates and counts.

Ask questions, such as "Who can hold the most/least?", "Who do you think has the largest/smallest hand?"

Numerals
pages 8–9

Numbers are used all around us in everyday life: on television programmes, house numbers, buses, cars, in prices on goods. Your child will be able to read small numbers and then, with help, the larger numbers. As you walk along the street, read the numbers that you see to each other.

Number frieze

You will need:
A4 size paper;
Felt pens;
Coloured sticky paper;
Sticky tape.

Your child can write the numeral at the top and the number word at the bottom of each sheet. In the middle she can stick the corresponding number of cutout shapes. When the sheets are finished they can be joined on the back with sticky tape and then put up as a frieze.

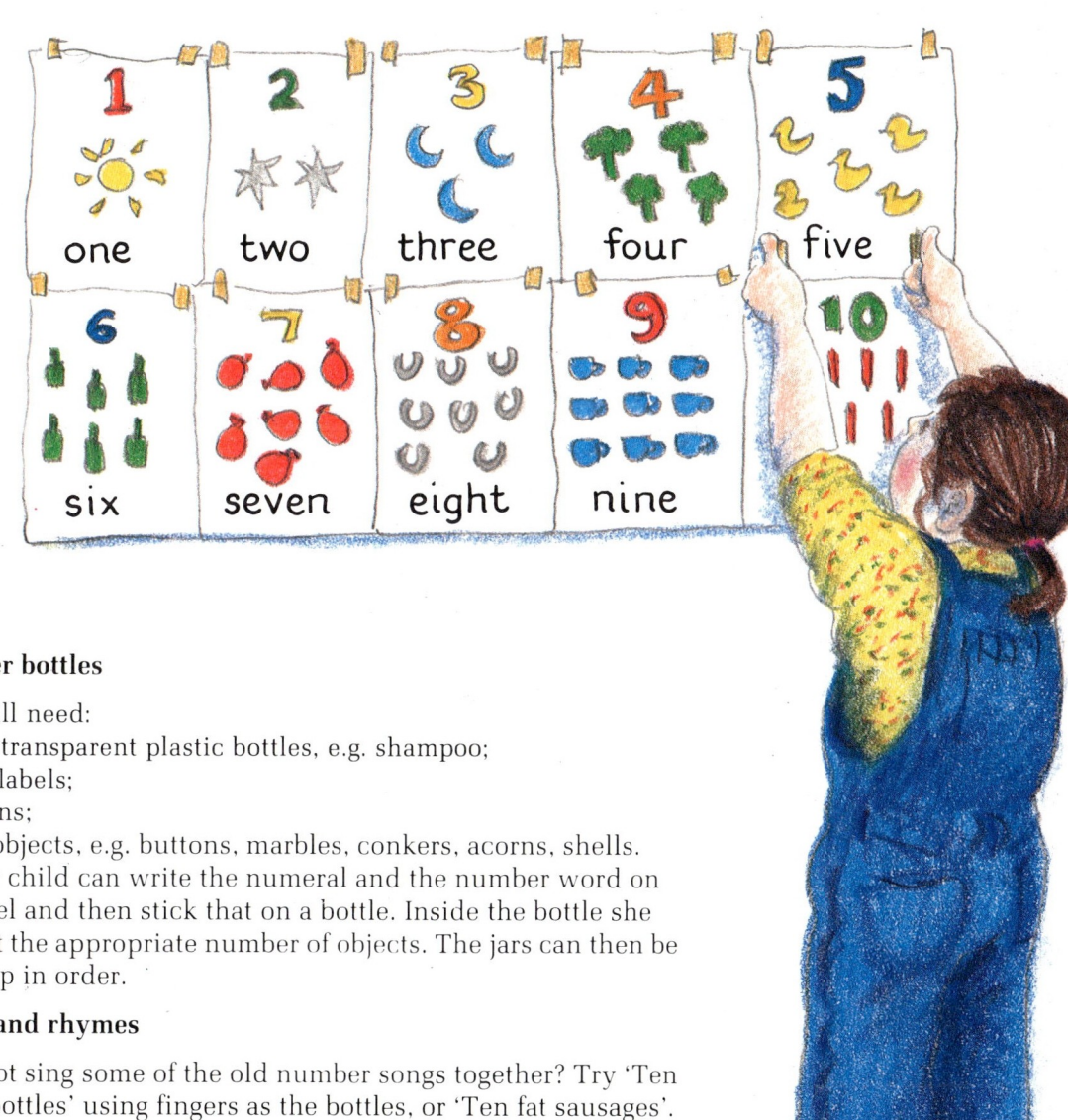

Number bottles

You will need:
Empty transparent plastic bottles, e.g. shampoo;
Sticky labels;
Felt pens;
Small objects, e.g. buttons, marbles, conkers, acorns, shells.

Your child can write the numeral and the number word on the label and then stick that on a bottle. Inside the bottle she can put the appropriate number of objects. The jars can then be lined up in order.

Songs and rhymes

Why not sing some of the old number songs together? Try 'Ten green bottles' using fingers as the bottles, or 'Ten fat sausages'. These songs will help your child to remember number order and to count forwards and backwards.

Number patterns
pages 28–31

Playing games such as dominoes will help your child to begin to remember number bonds and to begin to find strategies for playing games and for solving problems.

Sevens

You will need a pack of dominoes (six as the highest number).

Up to four people can play this game. Share the dominoes between you. Take it in turns to lay a domino so that the total is 7. Start with double 6. Discuss with your child how to make a seven. "How many do we need?" Or "How many more do we need?"

There are many opportunities for making repeating patterns in the book, for example, threading alternate red and blue beads. Take opportunities to look at and talk about the repeating patterns that are in your home. There will be wallpaper patterns, patterns on jumpers, patterns on fancy socks.

When you and your child are listening to music, try clapping or tapping to the rhythms.

Shape and space attainment targets 9,10,11

3D shapes, 2D shapes, direction and location
pages 6–7, 8–9, 20–21, 31

There are many words that we use to describe the position of something, e.g. up, down, in, out, under, over, through, between, in front of, behind. Encourage you child to use these words as you or she are doing things, so that she understands the meaning.

Follow my leader

Line up one behind the other; each person copies what the leader does. The leader should use the correct word as she moves, e.g. "I'm going through this doorway."

Empty cardboard boxes and tubes make excellent junk materials for children to make models. This helps your child to learn about the shapes of the boxes and tubes and what she can do with them – which ones will build, which roll, which slide, how many faces they have, etc. Exciting models can be made which can also be painted. If your child finds that the cardboard won't take paint, the boxes can be unstuck along their seams, turned inside out and stuck together again. They will need a few hours to dry.

Modelling

You will need:
Junk boxes and tubes;
Child-safe strong glue (e.g. water-soluble PVA);
Safety scissors;
Paints;
Pencil;
Bottle tops, scraps of materials, pieces of foil for decoration.

Encourage your child to talk about the model that she is making. Can she name the shapes that she is using/making, e.g. cylinder, cone, cube, cuboid?

Your child will gradually begin to recognise and name the flat shapes: square, circle, rectangle, triangle. These are found not just in pictures but as the faces of solid shapes and as the faces of doors or windows for example. In the book, your child will have the opportunity to find and draw the faces of many everyday objects, for example, the flat screen of the television is rectangular.

Shape walk

When you go for a walk, look at the houses that you pass. Ask your child what shape the doors and windows are; what about the chimney pots, post boxes, gates?

Why not count how many rectanglar shapes you see, or how many circles? When you get home your child might draw a picture showing all the rectangles or circles seen on the walk.

Measures attainment targets 1 and 8

Volume and weight
pages 18–19, 22, 26–27

There is a recipe in the book which, with your help, your child should be able to make. These recipes encourage your child to measure proportion by volume.

When you are weighing out ingredients in the kitchen let your child help you. Show her how to get the scales to balance, if using a pan and weights scale, or how to measure using a dial.

When shopping in the supermarket let your child weigh out the loose vegetables and fruit.

Time

Telling the time

Throughout the book your child will find that there are clocks showing various times. Your child will see clocks with and without numbers and with Roman numbers. Help your child, when you see a clock, by saying what the time is.

There are many words which we use to express time: day, month, year, the days of the week, months of the year, yesterday, today, tomorrow, etc. Help your child to understand these by talking about them and encouraging your child to use them. Watch for the changing seasons. Keep a weather chart or a birthday chart so that you and your child discuss the passing of time.

Time walk

A walk in a town centre will give you an opportunity to point out all sorts of different clocks. There will be the town clock, the church clock, the jewellers with a window full of clocks and watches.

Capacity

pages 22, 26–27

Bath time can be fun time and learning time. You will find it helpful to collect empty plastic containers for using in the bath.

Bath time order

You will need: empty plastic bottle, yogurt pot, margarine tub.

First, both of you try to estimate which container will hold most and least. Then put them in order of what you think they will be, from least to most.

Now let your child pour water from one to another to check your order. Were you both right? Estimating improves with practice! Try making a chart of what you estimated and what you found by pouring.

Length

pages 14–15

Encourage your child to estimate and to compare lengths. Who has the longest/shortest stride? Who is wearing the longest scarf? A height measuring chart pinned to a wall will help your child to see how much she has grown and to see her height compared with other family members.

Make a measuring snake

You will need:
Empty cotton reels;
Long shoe lace;
Bodkin;
Scraps of fabric;
Scraps of coloured card;
Felt pens;
Strong, safe glue.

Thread the shoe lace onto the bodkin. Now your child can thread the cotton reels onto the shoe lace. The first and last can be tied on to stop them falling off. The first and last cotton reels can be decorated with felt pens or bits of fabric or card stuck on to make the face and the end of the tail.

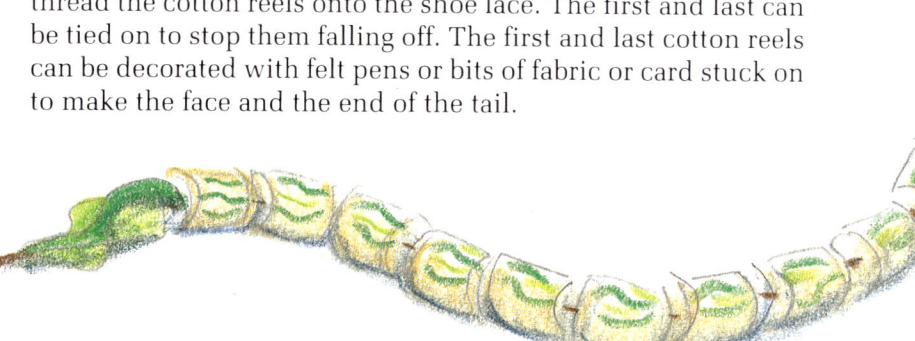

The snake can now be used to measure items around the home. Encourage your child to estimate first and then to measure, looking for things that are longer than, about the same as, or shorter than the snake. A chart can be made.

Encourage your child to talk about what she has found. Encourage her to use long, longer, longest, tall, taller, tallest, etc.

Money

pages 16–17

When you and your child are out shopping, let your child give the money to the sales assistant on occasions. If she has pocket money, give it to her using different coins each week so that she begins to understand the equivalent value of coins.

Simple shop games, as suggested in the book, may quite easily be set up at home. Ask her questions about the coins, "Can you find another way of giving me 5p?", for example.

Handling data attainment targets, 9, 12, 13, 14

Data handling
pages 12–13

Encourage your child to keep charts, for example, a weather chart, a chart for the family's favourite TV programmes, a chart showing what she has done each day. These can be drawings or pictures stuck onto paper. Charts showing "how many" or "how much" or "how long" can be kept.

Foot size chart

You will need:
Paper to draw feet on;
Pencil;
Safety scissors;
Large sheet of paper;
Paper glue.

Your child can draw round the foot of each member of the family, cut out the drawing and stick them onto the chart. Ask questions such as "Who has the longest/shortest foot?" and "How can you tell from the chart who has the shortest/longest foot?"

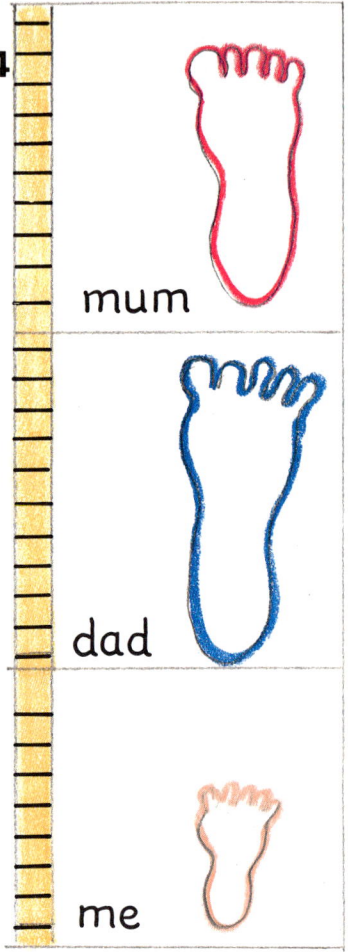

Probability

Talk about the things that will happen, that won't happen, that might happen.
"It will be dark tonight."
"One day I shall be as tall as a double decker bus."
"We shall go to the seaside."
Help your child to appreciate that some things may/may not happen, e.g. "It will rain tomorrow."

Button bag game

You will need:
10 buttons of one colour;
10 buttons of another colour;
Strong paper bag;
Paper to keep a chart;
Pencil.

Together, count the buttons into the bag. Now let your child guess what colour the first button she takes out of the bag will be. Keep a record, first guessing then drawing out a button. Put the button back after each go and give the bag a good shake. Try this ten times. Your child should begin to see that there is no set pattern to this; the buttons will be drawn out at random.

Peter and his friend are thirsty. Dad shows them how to make a fruit drink.

slices of orange, apple and banana

orange juice

apple juice

fizzy lemonade

Peter mixes all the ingredients together in a large jug then pours it into glasses.

Ask if you can weigh some things at home.

The Cat and Mouse Game

Help the mouse to find the cheese.

He can go up, down, left and right.

How many different ways can you find?

 **left**

up ⬆

right ➡

down ⬇

If you have a sandpit, you could try to find out which of your buckets or shapes holds the most sand.

1.

How many?

2.

I made a good guess.

Why don't you guess the number of some things?

Check to see if you are right.

Peter loves to pour water from one pot to another.

Do you think all the water in the red pot will fit into the green one?

26

How many spoonfuls of water fill the egg cup?

"These are even numbers."

2 4 6 8 10

2
4
6

Can you make this pattern bigger?
What is the next number?

Make the pattern with buttons.

These are odd numbers.

1 3 5 7 9

Can you make this pattern bigger?
Try to draw it.

Try to make some patterns for yourself.

What colour bead will Peter thread next?

Make up some patterns using only red and blue beads.

Draw the patterns.

Can you make a printed pattern
like this one?

Make a paper-children chain.
Can you colour the children
to make a pattern?

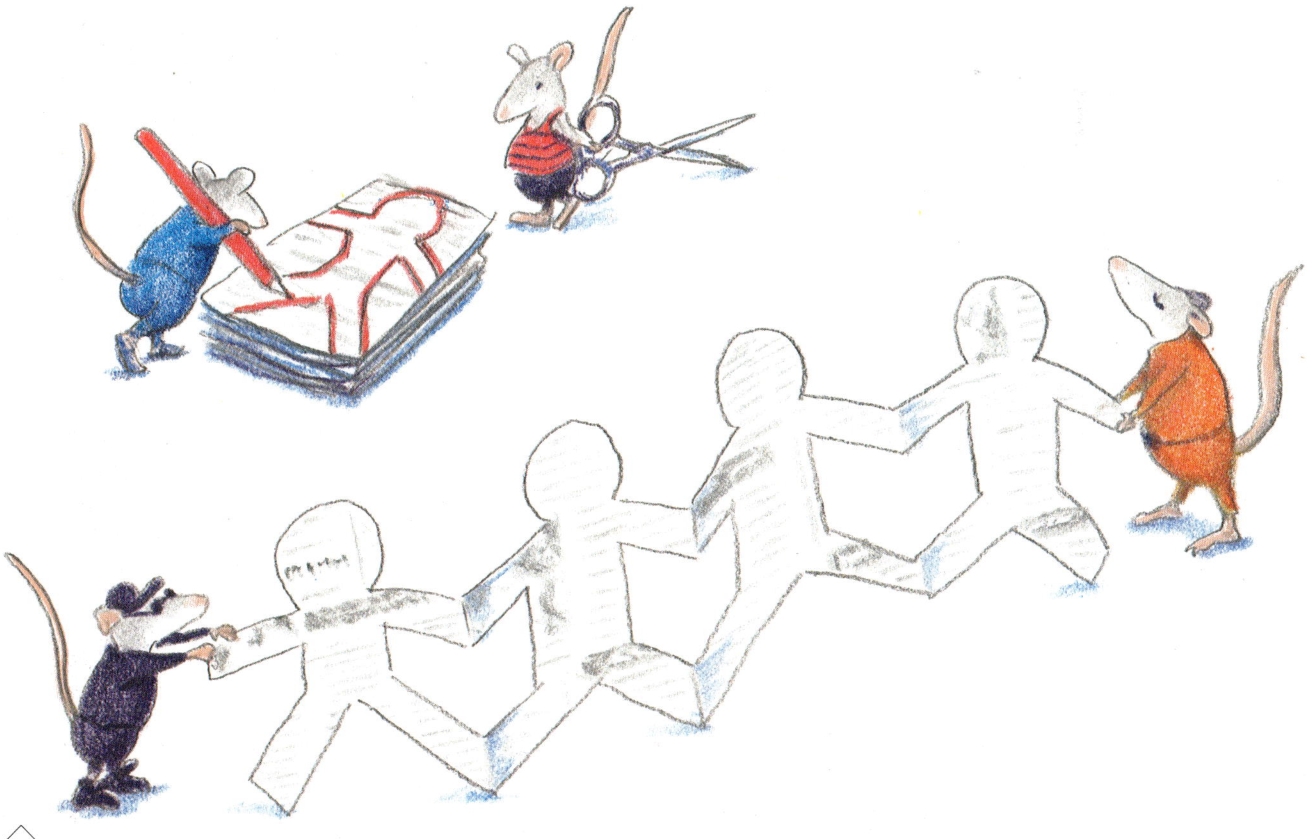

How many stairs does Peter have to climb?